FALCONS

BIRDS OF PREY

BY NATHAN SOMMER

BELLWETHER MEDIA • MINNEAPOLIS, MN

EPIC BOOKS are no ordinary books. They burst with intense action, high-speed heroics, and shadows of the unknown. Are you ready for an Epic adventure?

This edition first published in 2019 by Bellwether Media, Inc.

Library of Congress Cataloging-in-Publication Data

Names: Sommer, Nathan, author.
Title: Falcons / by Nathan Sommer.
Description: Minneapolis, MN : Bellwether Media, Inc., 2019. | Series: Epic.
   Birds of Prey | Audience: Age 7-12. | Audience: Grade 2 to 7. | Includes
   bibliographical references and index.
Identifiers: LCCN 2018003559 (print) | LCCN 2018006813 (ebook) | ISBN
   9781626178793 (hardcover : alk. paper) | ISBN 9781681036250 (ebook)
Subjects: LCSH: Falcons–Juvenile literature. | Birds of prey–Juvenile
   literature.
Classification: LCC QL696.F34 (ebook) | LCC QL696.F34 S66 2019 (print) | DDC
   598.9/6–dc23
LC record available at https://lccn.loc.gov/2018003559

TABLE OF CONTENTS

A STUNNING DIVE

The peregrine falcon rises into the sky.
This quick **predator** finds **prey** from high up.

The falcon spots a pheasant a mile away. It flies closer. Then, it dives at 200 miles (322 kilometers) per hour!

The World's Fastest

Peregrine falcons have hit speeds of 242 miles (389 kilometers) per hour. They are the fastest animals ever recorded!

The falcon strikes the pheasant feetfirst. It **dazes** the prey!

The falcon catches its meal with its **talons** and lands. It digs in with its toothlike beak. Most prey are no match for the speedy falcon!

WHAT ARE FALCONS?

GYRFALCON

Falcons are some of the fastest birds on Earth. There are more than 35 kinds of them worldwide.

These midsize birds of prey have long, pointed wings and tails. Many have helmetlike markings on their faces.

TYPES OF FALCONS

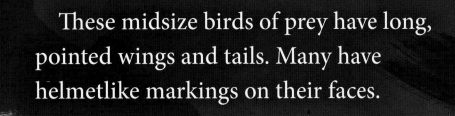

PEREGRINE FALCON

MERLIN

GYRFALCON

COMMON KESTREL

Falcons are common birds of prey.
They **adapt** to all types of **habitats.**

Arctic Predators

Falcons even live at the North Pole! There, gyrfalcons hunt seabirds and baby Arctic foxes.

COMMON KESTRELS

These birds prefer open spaces and high **perches** near water. In cities, they often nest on skyscrapers!

SPEED DEMONS

AMUR FALCON

Falcons often eat other birds. Some attack birds bigger than them in midair!

Insects, **rodents**, and lizards are also favorite foods. Falcons sneak up on them. They fly close to the ground.

AMERICAN KESTREL

Making a Comeback

In the 1940s, many farms used a harmful bug spray. The spray killed many falcons. In 1972, this bug spray was banned. Then, falcon numbers grew again!

13

SAKER FALCON

Falcons hunt from high perches. Then, they attack prey in a quick, steep dive. Some falcons **stoop** from 3,000 feet (914 meters)!

Their speed can kill prey in one strike.

Birds of Sport

People have hunted with falcons for centuries. The birds catch prey. Then they bring it back to their humans!

15

EURASIAN HOBBY

Falcons are shaped to fly fast. Their wings and bodies are long and pointed. This makes the birds extra **aerodynamic**.

Little cones in their beaks help
falcons breathe while they dive.
The birds can beat their wings
at high speeds without tiring!

CONE

PRAIRIE FALCON

Falcons use their beaks to weaken food.
Their beaks are sharper and more toothlike
than most birds of prey.

The birds often bite into necks midair. That way, these speedy hunters can eat on the go!

GYRFALCON PROFILE

RED LIST STATUS: LEAST CONCERN

LEAST CONCERN	NEAR THREATENED	VULNERABLE	ENDANGERED	CRITICALLY ENDANGERED	EXTINCT IN THE WILD	EXTINCT

AVERAGE LIFE SPAN: ABOUT 13 YEARS
GREATEST HUNTING TOOL: SPEED
WINGSPAN: 4 FEET (1.2 METERS)
TOP SPEED: UP TO 130 MILES (209 KILOMETERS) PER HOUR

GYRFALCON RANGE MAP

GYRFALCON
RANGE =

PREY

| PHEASANTS | MAGPIES | PTARMIGANS | HARES |

GLOSSARY

adapt—to change over time to more easily survive

aerodynamic—able to move through the air quickly and easily

dazes—knocks senseless with a blow

habitats—the homes or areas where animals prefer to live

perches—high places where birds watch for prey, such as branches or rooftops

predator—an animal that hunts other animals for food

prey—animals that are hunted by other animals for food

rodents—small mammals that gnaw on their food; mice, squirrels, and beavers are all rodents.

stoop—to dive at very high speeds

talons—the strong, sharp claws of falcons and other birds of prey

TO LEARN MORE

At the Library

Hamilton, S.L. *Falcons*. Minneapolis, Minn.: Abdo Publishing, 2017.

Herrington, Lisa M. *Built for Speed: Catch Up with Cheetahs, Falcons, and Other Fast Movers*. New York, N.Y.: Children's Press, 2018.

Plattner, Josh. *Peregrine Falcon*. Minneapolis, Minn.: Super Sandcastle, 2016.

On the Web

Learning more about falcons is as easy as 1, 2, 3.

1. Go to www.factsurfer.com.

2. Enter "falcons" into the search box.

3. Click the "Surf" button and you will see a list of related web sites.

With factsurfer.com, finding more information is just a click away.

INDEX